GUNG HAY FAT CHOY
恭　喜　發　財

GUNG HAY FAT CHOY

恭 喜 發 財

HAPPY NEW YEAR

Festivals and Holidays

By June Behrens

Photographs Compiled by Terry Behrens

SCHOLASTIC INC.

New York   Toronto   London   Auckland   Sydney
Mexico City   New Delhi   Hong Kong   Buenos Aires

TO JOHN YEE
of the Chinese Historical Society of California

ACKNOWLEDGMENTS

The author wishes to acknowledge with thanks the assistance of John Yee, and Judy and Johnson Yee. Others who helped to make this manuscript possible include members of the Ba family: Larry and Amy Ba, and their children Allen, Lorita, Linda, and Alice.

PHOTO CREDITS

Cover Photograph: View-Master International Group
Chinese New Year parade: Ronnie Ramos

Copyright © 1982 by Regensteiner Publishing Enterprises, Inc.
All rights reserved. Published by Scholastic Inc., 555 Broadway, New York, NY 10012.
Printed in the U.S.A.

ISBN 0-516-24102-8

4   5   6   7   8   9   10   61   10 09 08 07 06 05 04 03

GUNG HAY FAT CHOY
恭 喜 發 財

GUNG HAY FAT CHOY!

A fierce dragon leaps and weaves from side to side. Strings of firecrackers explode in midair. We hear the sounds of gongs and clashing cymbals. What an exciting and noisy parade!

GUNG HAY FAT CHOY means
best wishes and congratulations. Have
a prosperous and good year.

It is the Chinese New Year. This
joyous festival may last many days. It is
a time for family reunions, for honoring
ancestors, and thanking the gods for
their blessings.

It is a celebration of the birth of a new year. The new year festival and parade is a very special time for the Chinese.

The Chinese add a year to their age on New Year's Day, no matter when they were born.

This is the grandest birthday party of all!

Chinese New Year does not come at the same time every year. The date may fall any time between mid-January and mid-February. Chinese festivals are celebrated according to dates on the ancient Chinese lunar calendar.

It is called the lunar calendar because the length of the months are decided by the cycles of the moon.

Each new Chinese year is given the name of an animal. It is named after one of the 12 animal symbols on the Chinese zodiac. These animal symbols date back thousands of years.

It is said that a person born within an animal's year will have the qualities of that animal. Chinese learn their future and fortunes by the animal symbols of the Chinese zodiac.

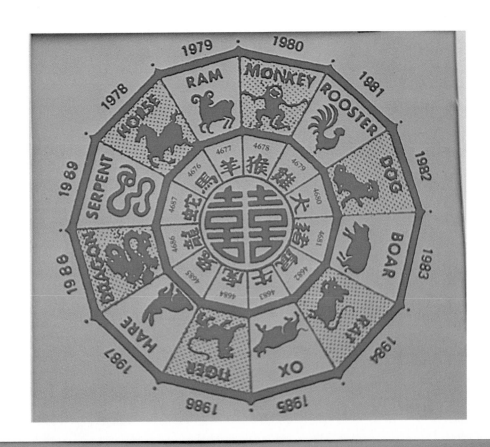

THE CHINESE LUNAR CALENDAR
Horoscope

RAT		RABBIT	
1900	1972	1903	1975
1912	1984	1915	1987
1924	1996	1927	1999
1936	2008	1939	2011
1948	2020	1951	2023
1960	2032	1963	2035

OX		DRAGON	
1901	1973	1904	1976
1913	1985	1916	1988
1925	1997	1928	2000
1937	2009	1940	2012
1949	2021	1962	2024
1961	2033	1964	2036

TIGER		SNAKE	
1902	1974	1905	1977
1914	1986	1917	1989
1926	1998	1929	2001
1938	2010	1941	2013
1950	2022	1963	2025
1962	2034	1965	2037

HORSE		Rooster	
1906	1978	1909	1981
1918	1990	1921	1993
1930	2002	1933	2005
1942	2014	1945	2017
1954	2026	1957	2029
1966	2038	1969	2041

Ram		DOG	
1907	1979	1910	1982
1919	1991	1922	1994
1931	2003	1934	2006
1943	2015	1946	2018
1955	2027	1958	2030
1967	2039	1970	2042

MONKEY		BOAR	
1908	1980	1911	1983
1920	1992	1923	1995
1932	2004	1935	2007
1944	2016	1947	2019
1956	2028	1959	2031
1968	2040	1971	2043

WHICH YEAR WERE YOU BORN ?

Chinese families make great
preparations for this special time of
year. Before the new year families
settle old debts and buy new clothes.
The house is cleaned and food is
prepared.

Homes are filled with flowers and fruit. Families display pyramids of oranges and apples. An apple is a symbol of good luck for the new year.

Oranges and apples are picked for a special reason. The Chinese believe red and orange are colors of joy. You will see the colors of joy everywhere at the Chinese New Year Festival!

There are red and orange scrolls everywhere. The Chinese characters on the scrolls carry messages of Good Health, Luck, Long Life, Prosperity, Happiness.

On the eve of the new year, Chinese
families celebrate at a reunion dinner.
Offerings are made to family ancestors.
Sometimes doors and windows are
sealed with red, good luck papers.

Children stay awake as long as they
can on New Year's Eve. It is said that
the longer one stays up, the longer
one's parents will live.

The new year is a time for gift giving. Before midnight the children receive a special present, called *lai see*. It is good luck money wrapped in red paper.

Then, all of a sudden, there is a deafening explosion of firecrackers. It is the new year. Firecrackers will scare away lazy and evil spirits!

恭喜發財
GUNG HAY FAT CHOY

On New Year's morning the good luck seals on doors and windows are broken. On this day one must be very careful, according to custom. What happens the first day of the year may decide the events for the coming year.

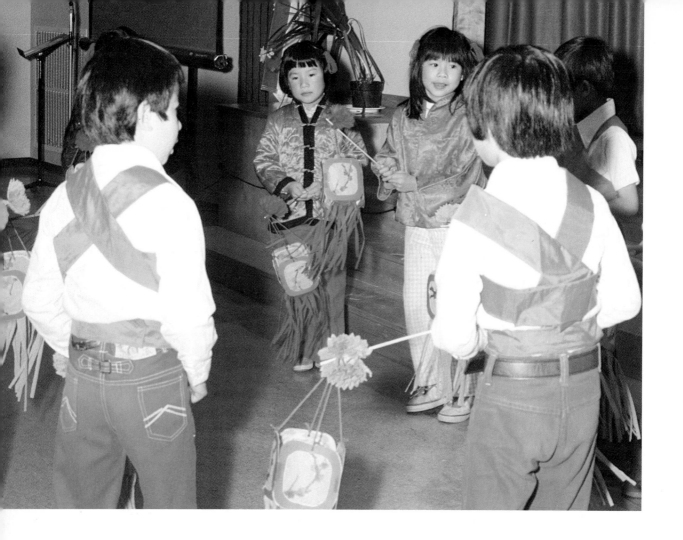

Everyone takes care to say and do the right things. Everyone wears new clothes and thinks good thoughts and speaks kind words. Respects are paid to honored ancestors. Everywhere you will hear GUNG HAY FAT CHOY!

   Days of celebration follow the first
day of the Chinese new year! The
festival may last as long as seven days.
Chinatown is alive with color and
activity, sounds, and wonderful smells.
   At the community carnival we watch
Tai Chi, Chinese boxing, lion dancing,
and opera. There are traditional dances,
art exhibits, karate contests, and
delicious foods at the school fair.

Here come the lion dancers! They're
dancing to the beat of a giant drum.
Gongs and cymbals at first are loud and
fast. The beat becomes slower as the
lion turns and twists and dances.
Chinese poets wrote about the lion
dance over 1,000 years ago.

Dancers carry the comical papier-mâché head of a lion. They dance in front of places of business and homes. Owners who come out and offer the lion a donation are blessed with joy and good fortune.

The grandest show of all is the Golden Dragon Parade in the evening. The fierce, bright-eyed dragon with so many legs leads the parade.

The Chinese dragon is a most sacred animal and was the emblem of the Chinese emperors. It is a symbol of strength and goodness. Once each year the dragon appears to wish everyone peace, prosperity, and good luck.

Back up! Firecrackers are exploding everywhere. The dragon is weaving back and forth.

Sometimes the dragon chases a
round object. If the object is red, it is a
flaming sun. If it is white, the dragon is
chasing a great pearl, which brings
power.

What a parade! Here comes the
children's lantern procession. Lanterns
are of all sizes and shapes and colors.
Look at the weapon bearers and the
musicians. More fireworks!

Let's thank our Chinese American friends for sharing a part of their culture with us. We have eaten steamed shrimps and were given oranges for good luck. We watched a Tai Chi exercise and saw an opera. We made a Chinese character, which is a word.

HAPPY

NEW

YEAR

We even learned to say some
Chinese words.
GUNG HAY FAT CHOY!

The Chinese New Year is a time of rejoicing, family reunions, gift giving, and feasting. It is a birthday party for everyone.

Chinese families who are residents of Chinatowns in major cities in the United States meet in their respective communities in late January or early February to celebrate their new year. Everyone is invited to join them and share in their celebration.

A highlight of the celebration is the symbolic Dragon Parade. Grand lion dancers and children's lantern processions are a part of the festivities, with magnificent and deafening fireworks displays to help bring in the new year.

JUNE BEHRENS has written more than fifty books, plays, and film-strips for young people, touching on all subject areas of the school curriculum. Her interest and travels in China inspired GUNG HAY FAT CHOY, the second title in the Festivals and Holidays Series. Mrs. Behrens has for many years been an educator in one of California's largest public school systems. She is a graduate of the University of California at Santa Barbara and has a Master's degree from the University of Southern California. Mrs. Behrens is listed in Who's Who of American Women. She is a recipient of the Distinguished Alumni Award from the University of California for her contributions in the field of education. She and her husband live in Rancho Palos Verdes, a Southern California suburb.